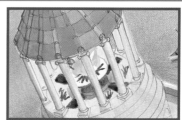

WONDERS

of the

WORLD

Written and illustrated by

MARK BERGIN

Created and designed by

DAVID SALARIYA

W
FRANKLIN WATTS
A Division of Grolier Publishing
NEW YORK • LONDON • HONG KONG • SYDNEY
DANBURY, CONNECTICUT

Contents

Ancient and Modern Wonders

Ever since the invention of writing people have compiled lists of the world's most impressive sights and buildings. The most famous of these buildings are called the Seven Wonders of the World.

A Greek writer, Antipater of Sidon, made the first known list over 2,000 years ago. It included the most outstanding buildings and structures of his day in the ancient world.

The sites of the Seven Wonders of the Ancient World.

Statue of Zeus

Mausoleum of Halicarnassus

Temple of Artemis

Colossus of Rhodes

Pharos of Alexandria

Pyramids of Giza

Hanging Gardens of Babylon

The number seven was thought to have mystical or religious significance, which is why the number of wonders was limited to seven. No one now knows the purpose of Antipater's list, but the buildings on it show us just how good the people of the ancient world were at engineering.

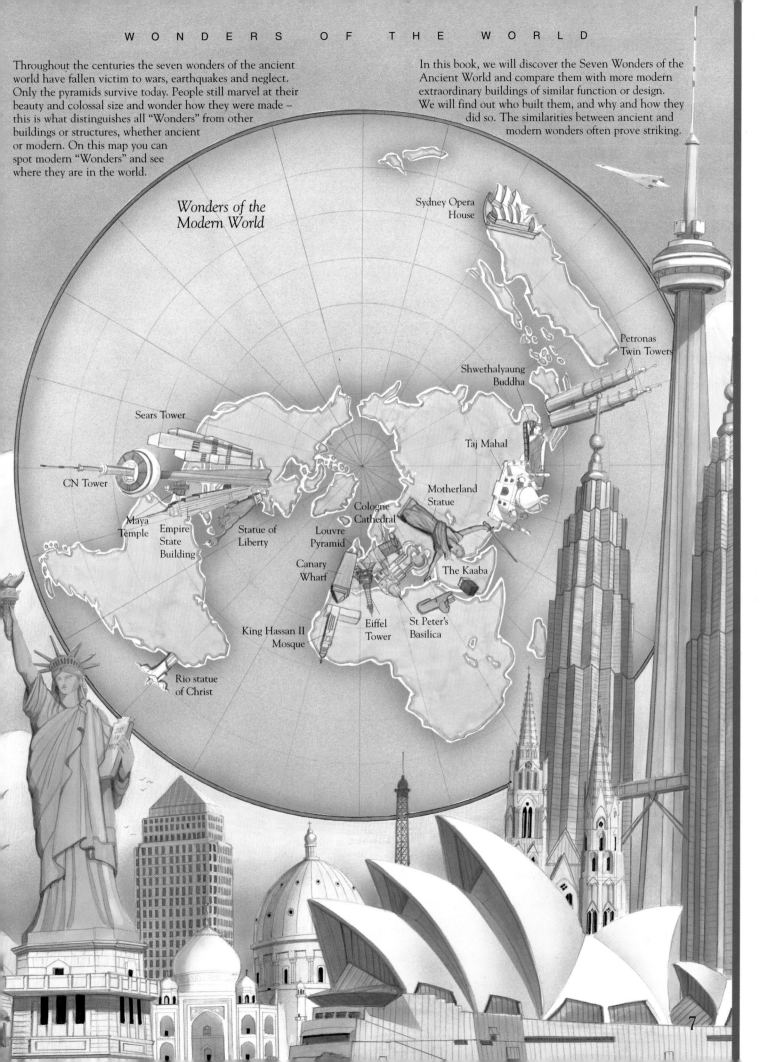

Throughout the centuries the seven wonders of the ancient world have fallen victim to wars, earthquakes and neglect. Only the pyramids survive today. People still marvel at their beauty and colossal size and wonder how they were made – this is what distinguishes all "Wonders" from other buildings or structures, whether ancient or modern. On this map you can spot modern "Wonders" and see where they are in the world.

In this book, we will discover the Seven Wonders of the Ancient World and compare them with more modern extraordinary buildings of similar function or design. We will find out who built them, and why and how they did so. The similarities between ancient and modern wonders often prove striking.

Wonders of the Modern World

Sydney Opera House

Petronas Twin Towers

Shwethalyaung Buddha

Sears Tower

Taj Mahal

Motherland Statue

CN Tower

Cologne Cathedral

Maya Temple

Empire State Building

Statue of Liberty

Louvre Pyramid

The Kaaba

Canary Wharf

King Hassan II Mosque

Eiffel Tower

St Peter's Basilica

Rio statue of Christ

Pyramids of Giza

The Pyramids at Giza have cast their shadow across the sands of Egypt for over 5,000 years. They were built as tombs for the pharaohs of ancient Egypt and are the oldest of the Seven Wonders of the World. The ancient Egyptians believed that after death a pharaoh's body had to be preserved or his spirit would die. Each pyramid was designed to protect a pharaoh's body forever. In building the pyramids, the Egyptians hoped for everlasting prosperity by providing a fitting dwelling for the pharaoh and his possessions. Once in the afterlife, reunited with the sun god Re, the pharaoh would then look favorably on them. The shape of a pyramid is thought to represent the sun's rays falling from heaven to earth.

Above: After the site was leveled, a grid of channels was dug.

Right: The grand gallery and the burial chambers of Cheops and the queen were deep in the pyramid.

Above: Before construction began, the grid of channels was filled with water to show whether or not the surface of the site was level.

Starting at each corner, ramps were built against the side of each face of the pyramid. The ramps were extended as the height of the pyramid increased.

Nile riverboats carried stone – from the granite quarry at Aswan and the limestone quarries at Tura and the Mugattam hills – to the site of the great pyramids on the Nile's west bank at Giza. From the bank the stones were dragged by teams of men along a causeway to the site, where skilled masons fitted them into place.

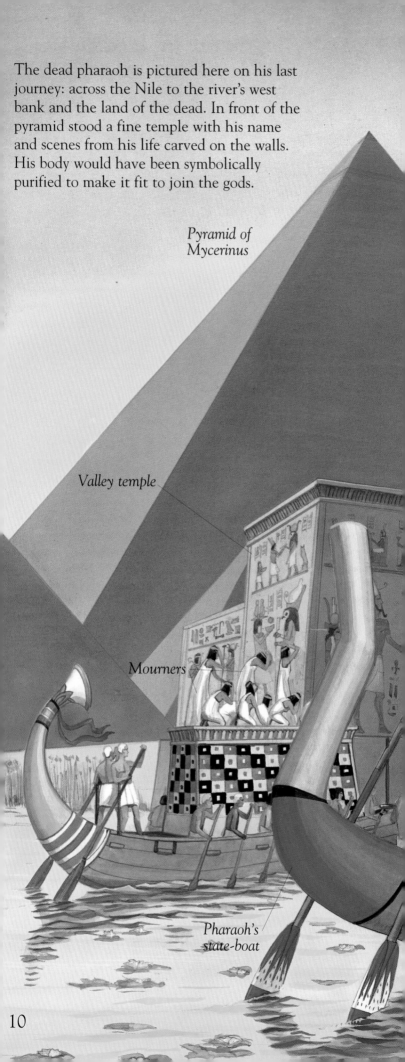

The dead pharaoh is pictured here on his last
journey: across the Nile to the river's west
bank and the land of the dead. In front of the
pyramid stood a fine temple with his name
and scenes from his life carved on the walls.
His body would have been symbolically
purified to make it fit to join the gods.

Pyramid of
Mycerinus

Valley temple

Mourners

Pharaoh's
state-boat

10

Death of the Pharaoh

A state-boat like the one below was found buried at the bottom of the pyramid of Cheops. It was made of cedar wood and was 147 ft (45 m) long. The stern-post was shaped like the Egyptians' traditional papyrus boats.

Right: Dating from A.D. 600-900, the 246 ft (75 m) high Jaguar temple built by the Mayans in their ancient religious center of Tikal (in Central America) towers above its surroundings. The colorful temple at the top of the stepped pyramid was reached by a grand stairway. Below: Pyramids still fascinate – this one at the Louvre, in Paris, France, was built in 1988.

Pyramid of Chephren

Pyramid of Cheops

Hanging Gardens of Babylon

The Hanging Gardens of Babylon are believed to have been built for Amytis, one of the wives of King Nebuchadnezzar in the 9th century B.C. The vast barren plain where Babylon stood (in what is now Iraq) made her homesick for the hills and leafy beauty of her homeland. So the King ordered the architect Semiramis to build terraced gardens within the city. To keep the gardens green throughout the long, hot summers, a system of hidden pipes brought water up from the nearby River Euphrates. When completed, the gardens would seem an exotic paradise rising from the desert. The royal family would walk the terraces where plants and aromatic flowers grew in abundance and palms and cypress trees gave shade from the burning heat.

Though the Hanging Gardens have long since vanished, gardens are still created as places to relax and admire nature. They have taken many forms, among them Japanese gravel gardens, geometric shapes in Renaissance Italy and the artificial "natural" landscapes of 18th-century England.

Above: The garden of the Taj Mahal, India, was laid out in a geometric design in the 17th century. The water in the central channels reflects the beauty of the building.
Below: In stark contrast is the simplicity of the Ryoanji garden in Kyoto, Japan. Made with rocks and raked gravel, it symbolizes Zen Buddhist thought.

Marco Polo visited Kublai Khan's Chinese palace gardens in 1279. He described them as full of specially chosen trees and beautiful animals with a huge lake stocked with fish.

In 18th-century England fashion moved away from the formal, geometric shapes of Renaissance gardens. Gardeners like Capability Brown redesigned the old gardens to create the effect of natural landscapes.

When Louis XIV built his palace at Versailles in France in the 17th century the gardens were laid out in geometric designs. The palace is surrounded by vast parklands and many beautiful gardens. Intricate flower beds, formal gardens, ornamental lakes, fountains and statues form the backdrop to one of the most glittering courts in Europe.

King Nebuchadnezzar's city of Babylon was protected by massive walls. It was one of the wealthiest cities in the ancient world – a center of trade and learning. Archeologists think that the Ziggurat, the pyramid-like temple devoted to Marduk the patron god of Babylon, may have been the fabled tower of Babel described in the Bible.

13

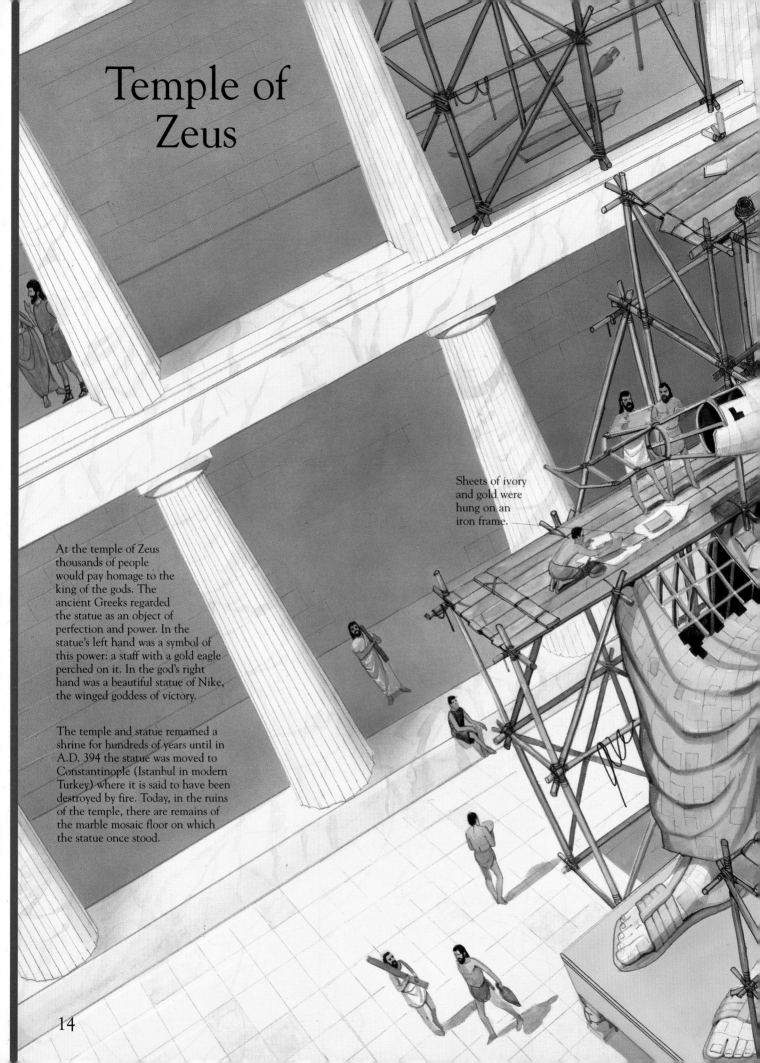

Temple of Zeus

At the temple of Zeus thousands of people would pay homage to the king of the gods. The ancient Greeks regarded the statue as an object of perfection and power. In the statue's left hand was a symbol of this power: a staff with a gold eagle perched on it. In the god's right hand was a beautiful statue of Nike, the winged goddess of victory.

The temple and statue remained a shrine for hundreds of years until in A.D. 394 the statue was moved to Constantinople (Istanbul in modern Turkey) where it is said to have been destroyed by fire. Today, in the ruins of the temple, there are remains of the marble mosaic floor on which the statue once stood.

Sheets of ivory and gold were hung on an iron frame.

Statue of
Nike

Burning incense

Offerings to
Zeus

16

Staff of power

Statue of Zeus

The ancient Greeks believed that Zeus, the king of the gods, lived on the top of Mount Olympus. It was one of the holiest places in Greece. At the foot of the mountain was the city of Olympia, famous for temples and the Games first held there in 776 B.C. The centerpiece of the city, the temple of Zeus was completed by 455 B.C. It took Phidias the sculptor another 22 years to complete the colossal statue of Zeus in the temple. The body was carved from ivory and the hair, beard, and drapery were made from gold sheets. Zeus's eyes were made with precious gemstones.

Below: Reconstruction of the temple of Zeus at Olympia.

Below: Millions of Muslims make the annual pilgrimage to Mecca, following the tradition that they should visit Islam's holy city at least once in their lifetime. The Kaaba, the holiest shrine, stands in the central courtyard of the mosque. In one of its walls is the sacred black stone which Mohammed, the founder of Islam, is said to have touched.

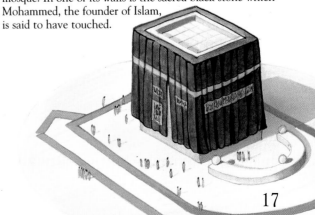

17

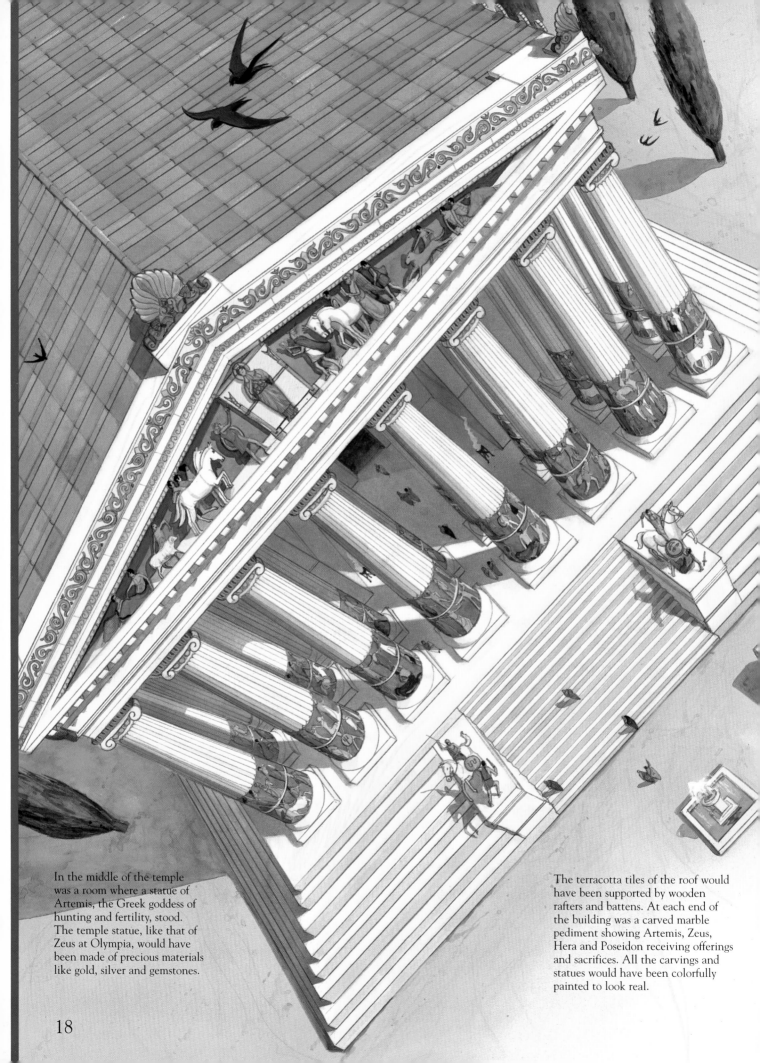

In the middle of the temple was a room where a statue of Artemis, the Greek goddess of hunting and fertility, stood. The temple statue, like that of Zeus at Olympia, would have been made of precious materials like gold, silver and gemstones.

The terracotta tiles of the roof would have been supported by wooden rafters and battens. At each end of the building was a carved marble pediment showing Artemis, Zeus, Hera and Poseidon receiving offerings and sacrifices. All the carvings and statues would have been colorfully painted to look real.

18

Temple of Artemis

The temple of Artemis at Ephesus (in modern Turkey) was built on the site of an earlier temple which was burned down in 356 B.C. by a madman called Herostratus. Many years later, Alexander the Great captured the city and decided to rebuild the temple. This took 120 years as it was one of the largest temples of its time – 171 ft (52 m) wide and 369 ft (112 m) long. Famed not only for its size, each of the 127 columns had at its base a decorated frieze, showing gods, heroes and mythical beasts.

Found in the jungle of Burma (now Myanmar) in 1881, this figure of Buddha is called the Shwethalyaung. It was discovered at the site of the ancient city of Pagan, and restored in 1946. Made in the 10th century B.C., the statue measures 180 ft (55 m) in length and 54 ft (16 m) in height.

In Morocco, the mosque of King Hassan II towers over the city of Casablanca. It is one of the largest mosques ever built and can hold up to 100,000 worshipers. At night its pink marble exterior is floodlit, so even after dark it still dominates the city.

Built on the site of the tomb of Peter the apostle, St Peter's in Rome, Italy, was built between 1506 and 1626. It has a 138 ft (42 m) dome and a colonnade that encircles the large piazza in front of the basilica. The cross on the dome soars to a height of 456 ft (138 m). This immense building was the largest church in the world until 1989, when the Basilica of Our Lady in the Ivory Coast, Africa, was completed.

Farmers in 1974 were digging a well near the Chinese city of Xian when they accidentally broke into a pit containing life-size terracotta statues of warriors. These were part of a 6,000-strong army guarding the tomb of the first Emperor, Qui Shi Hwang (259-209 B.C.). Horses, archers and 90 chariots were later found and traces of paint showed that originally all were painted to look lifelike. The site is so large that not all of it has yet been excavated.

The Taj Mahal near Agra in India was built in the 1630s by Shah Jahan, a Mogul emperor who was heartbroken at the death of his wife Mumtaz. The white marble tomb takes its name from his wife's title, Taj Mahal, the Crown of the Palace.

Mausoleum of Halicarnassus

In 354 B.C., above the city of Halicarnassus (in what is now south-western Turkey), a monument to a powerful ruler was nearing completion. Towering to a height of 147 ft (45 m), it was built in memory of King Mausolus of Caria under the supervision of his widow Artemisia. Although in ruins, much of the monument survived until the 15th century A.D., when it was finally destroyed by an earthquake. "Mausoleum," the modern word for a large and splendid tomb, comes from the name of this ancient king.

Following the practice of the time, construction of the tomb had started well before King Mausolus's death in 353 B.C. To finish it, Artemisia employed two of the best craftsmen in the Greek world: the architect Pythias and the sculptor Scopas. Pythias supervised the building of the temple on top of the tomb and Scopas oversaw the making of the many statues of gods and the king's family. He also made a frieze round the building which showed battles between the female warriors known as Amazons and Greek warriors. According to records written at the time, the monument took over 10 years to build using thousands of men. Crowning the building was a 9.5 ft (3 m) high marble statue showing Mausolus and Artemisia in a quadriga, a chariot drawn by four horses.

Statue of Mausolus and Artemisia in a marble chariot.

Pyramid-like roof

Temple

Tomb of Mausolus

21

The Colossus was made of thin sheets of bronze supported by an iron skeleton. It took over 10 years to build and was finally finished in 290 B.C. Large blocks of stone were used inside to weigh it down and keep it in place. However, this was the most short-lived "Wonder." In 224 B.C., an earthquake caused it to fall into the sea.

Colossus of Rhodes

The people of Rhodes built a statue of Helios the sun god in 300 B.C. This was to thank the god after they had successfully defended their island against an enemy invasion in 304 B.C. The statue was built in Lindos, Rhodes' main harbor, probably at the entrance. It was of a colossal size (hence the name Colossus) – around 123 ft (37 m) in height – and could be seen from far out at sea. It was built by Chares, who was a student of the Greek sculptor Lysippus.

Building giant statues is an ancient tradition. In Egypt, the Sphinx [60 ft (18 m) high and 240 ft (73 m) long] was originally built to guard the pyramids 5000 years ago. The Statue of Liberty [153 ft (46 m) high] has stood on an island in New York harbor since 1886. A 153 ft (40 m) high statue of Christ, built in 1931, towers over Rio de Janeiro, Brazil. The tallest of all is Motherland [270 ft (82 m)], built in 1967 outside Volgograd, Russia.

Observation
deck

Windows

Liberty's face is
10 ft (3 m) wide.

Over 300 sheets of copper,
3/32 in. (3 mm) thick,
cover the statue.

In her left hand Liberty holds a tablet inscribed July IV MDCCLXXVI (July 4, 1776), the date the United States declared its independence from Britain.

JULY IV MDCCLXXVI

Liberty is 153 ft (46 m) tall.

The base is 156 ft (47 m) high.

Statue of Liberty

The modern "Colossus" is the Statue of Liberty which stands on Bedloe Island off the southern tip of Manhattan Island. For over a hundred years its presence has welcomed returning Americans or immigrants seeking a new life. The idea for the statue was first discussed in 1865 at a dinner party, to commemorate the centenary of American independence from Britain. Twenty-one years later the statue was erected in New York harbor, a gift from the people of France to the people of the United States.

The crown on Liberty's head has seven spikes which represent the seven seas and continents of the world.

The statue is hollow: the copper sculpture is supported by four massive iron columns and an internal framework. This was designed by Gustave Eiffel who built the Eiffel Tower in Paris. Liberty measures 153 ft (46 m) from torch to toe, but with the stone pedestal rises to a height of 306 ft (93 m). She weighs 204 tons – the outer covering of copper making up nearly half this weight.

When Bartholdi, the sculptor, saw the site for his statue he thought Bedloe Island would be perfect. The star-shaped base was part of former Fort Wood. After the statue was erected, the island was renamed Liberty Island.

Pharos of Alexandria

The lighthouse of the city of Alexandria, Egypt, stood on the island of Pharos, close to the city's port. One of Alexander the Great's generals, Ptolemy I, ordered it built in the 3rd century B.C. Its architect and builder was Sostratus. Constructed of white marble in a series of tapered stories, it reached a height of 134 ft (122 m). At the summit a beacon burned day and night. The light was so bright it could be seen 30 miles (49 km) out to sea.

Completed in about 280 B.C., the lighthouse took 20 years to build and symbolized the power and glory of the Greek nation. Alexandria was the center of world trade and teaching at this time. Damaged by earthquakes – one in A.D. 796 caused major damage – the Pharos was finally destroyed by another in the 13th century.

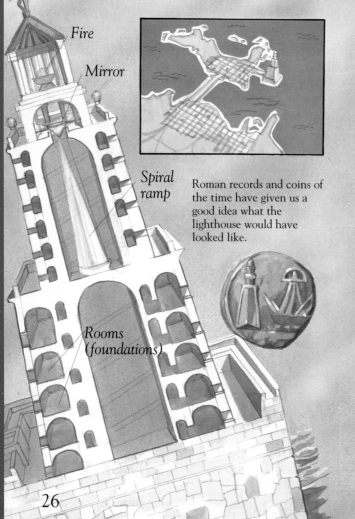

Fire

Mirror

Spiral ramp

Roman records and coins of the time have given us a good idea what the lighthouse would have looked like.

Rooms (foundations)

Small Greek ship heads out of Alexandria.

The lighthouse was built in three stages of vaulted masonry, each one tapering toward the top. The bottom section was square with many rooms with outward-facing windows. These were used to keep watch out to sea by day and by astronomers at night. The second story was octagonal and had a ramp around it which was used to carry the wood up to the beacon in the top, cylindrical section. Here a large concave mirror reflected and intensified the light of the beacon fire.

The Pharos took 20 years to build, and was completed in the reign of Ptolemy II.

Greek god
Helios

Concave mirror
to reflect light

Tall Towers

Today, tall towers dominate the skylines of the world's major cities. They still display wealth and the desire of the builders to create the tallest in the world. The Eiffel Tower in Paris, completed in 1889, was the world's tallest structure [990 ft (300 m)] until the construction of the Chrysler building in New York in 1930. This was quickly overshadowed by the Empire State Building, built in the same city and year, at 1,479 ft (449 m) tall. In 1974, the Sear's Tower, Chicago, pushed the record to 1,461 ft (443 m). Today, the Petronas Twin Towers in Malaysia hold the record at 1,491 ft (452 m). The CN Tower, Toronto, at 1,830 ft (555 m) is even taller, but is little more than a communications mast.

Causeway to city of Alexandria

High, walled platform protects from the action of the sea.

Empire State

Sears Tower

CN Tower

Petronas Towers

Eiffel Tower

Glossary

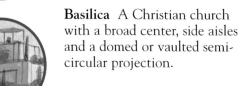

Archaeologist Person who studies ancient peoples and civilizations by digging up their remains.

Architect Designer of buildings.

Basilica A Christian church with a broad center, side aisles and a domed or vaulted semi-circular projection.

Battens Thin strips of wood which are used as reinforcements or supports.

Classical Based on order and tradition. Usually a term of praise.

Colossus Name given to very large statue. The Colossus of Rhodes was over 20 times life size.

Column A pillar or slender upright used as a support or an ornamental feature of a building.

Concrete Cement mixed with pebbles, crushed stone, sand and water to make a very strong building material. Concrete was first used by the Romans.

Dedicated Given to a god.

Dome A rounded vault forming a roof.

Foundations The base of a structure, often below ground level, carrying the weight of the building.

Frieze Horizontal band of decoration running around a building.

Hydraulic Operated by movement of water through pipes or channels.

Iron Metal of great strength.

Limestone White stone which is easy to carve. The Egyptian pyramids were built of limestone and granite.

Marble Hard, smooth, crystalline stone used for columns and sculptures.

Mausoleum The tomb of King Mausolus. It now means any large tomb.

Middle Ages Period of time between 1100-1500 A.D.

Moghul Term for 16th- and 17th- century Moghul Empire in India.

Mosaic Picture usually made up of small pieces of colored stone.

Next world Place a person's soul may go to after their death.

Offerings Gifts of food or artifacts offered to gods.

Pharaoh Name given to an Egyptian king. Its meaning is "great house" and comes from two Egyptian words, "per o."

Pharos Name of the lighthouse at Alexandria, taken from the island on which it stood. "Pharos" still means lighthouse in many languages.

Ramp Slope between the ground and a higher level.

Sacrifices Offerings to gods of food, wine or animals.

Shrine Place where a statue of a god or a holy relic is situated.

Sphinx Ancient Egyptian form of the sun god. Has the body of a lion and the head of the pharaoh.

Terrace Raised platform used for standing, walking, or growing things on.

Tomb Elaborate building with a grave at the center.

Ziggurat Type of stepped pyramidal structure built in ancient Mesopotamia.

Wonders of the World Facts

The Pharos of Alexandria was finished in 280 B.C. Its foundations still exist.

Cologne Cathedral in Germany was begun in 1248 and took two hundred years to complete. New towers were made in the 1860s and are the second highest in the world at 519 ft (157 m) tall.

The Basilica of St Peter's in Rome, Italy, was built between 1506 and 1626. Its huge dome rises to a height of over 453 ft (137 m) and until 1989 it was the largest church in the world. Since then a larger church built in the Ivory Coast has held this record.

The Eiffel Tower, Paris, was finished in 1889 and reaches a height of 990 ft (300 m). It was the world's tallest structure until 1930.

The Statue of Liberty, from the torch to the base of the stone pedestal, is almost 306 ft (93 m) high.

The Empire State building in Manhattan held the title of world's tallest building in 1930, at a height of 1,479 ft (449 m). It took just over a year to build.

The Motherland Statue in Russia holds the record as the world's largest full-figure statue, standing at 270 ft (82 m) high.

A 20th-century pyramid stands in front of the Louvre, Paris, on which

The pyramids of Giza were built between 2660-2560 B.C. The largest pyramid, at 486 ft (147 m), is still the world's largest stone structure.

The Hanging Gardens of Babylon in Iraq are estimated to have been 297 ft (90 m) high. The exact site of their location remains a mystery.

The Statue of Zeus at Olympia is said to have been 39 ft (12 m) high.

The Temple of Artemis was one of the largest temples of its time and was known for its friezes and sculptures. It may have been 369 ft (112 m) long and 171 ft (52 m) wide.

The Mausoleum of Halicarnassus towered to a height of 147 ft (45 m).

The Colossus of Rhodes was completed around 300 B.C. and was about 123 ft (37 m) high.

work began in the 15th century.

The Sydney Opera House in Australia is made up of a series of sail-like roofs. Designed by Jorn Utzon, it opened in 1973 having taken fourteen years to build.

The Basilica of Our Lady of Peace in the Ivory Coast, Africa, is the largest church in the world at 522 ft (158 m) high and 639 ft (193 m) long.

The Canary Wharf Tower in London is a 50-story skyscraper with a glass pyramid on the top. It is the tallest building in Britain at 738 ft (224 m) high.

The CN Tower in Toronto, Canada, finished in 1975, is the tallest free-standing structure in the world.

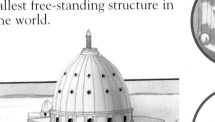

The tip of tallest antenna is 1,830 ft (555 m) above ground.

The Twin Petronas Towers in Kuala Lumpur, at 1491 ft (452 m), are the world's tallest buildings.

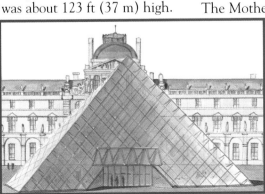

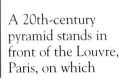

Index

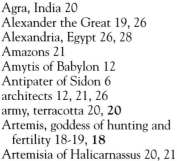